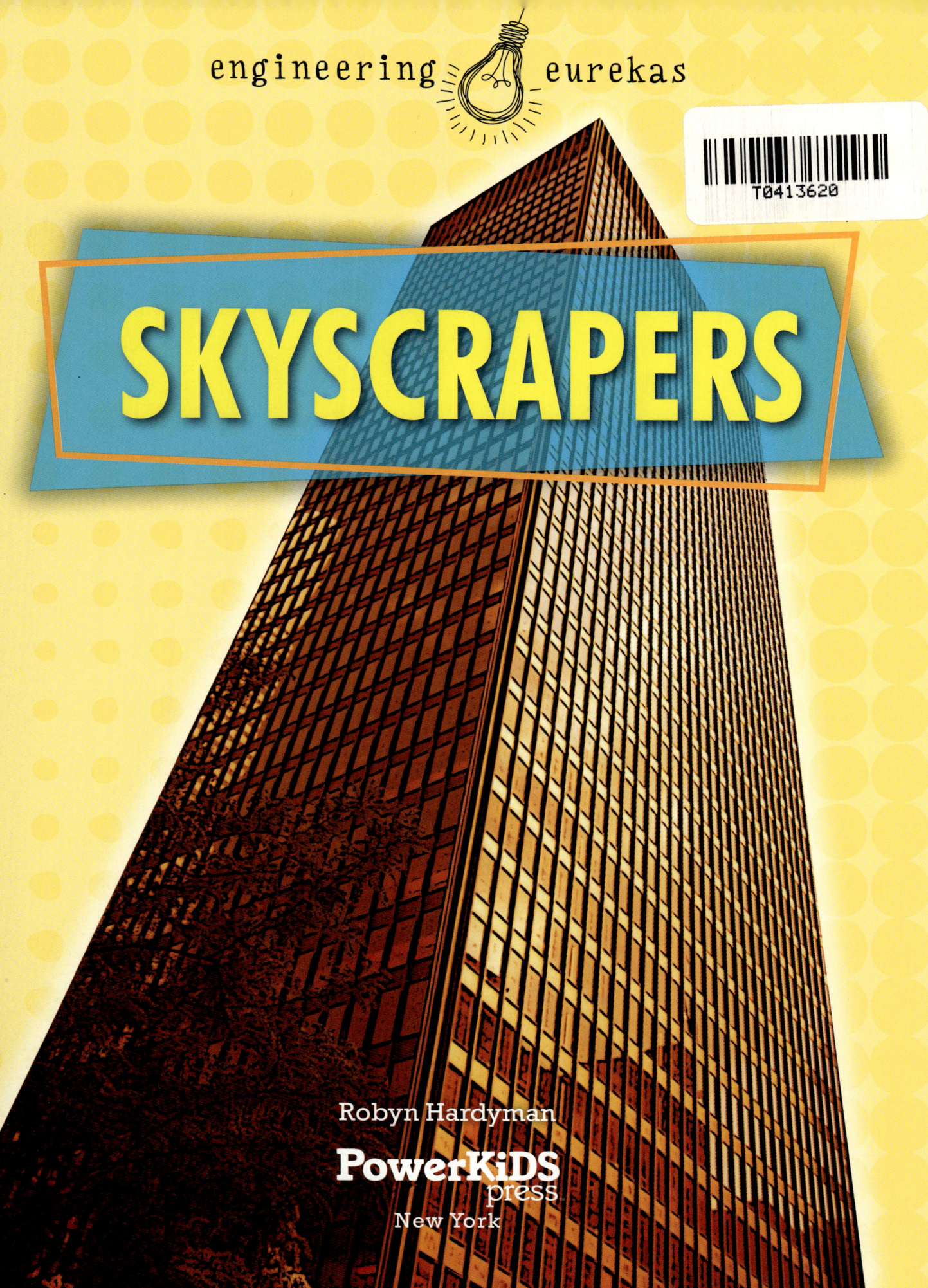

engineering eurekas

SKYSCRAPERS

Robyn Hardyman

PowerKiDS press
New York

Published in 2017 by
The Rosen Publishing Group, Inc.
29 East 21st Street, New York, NY 10010

Cataloging-in-Publication Data
Names: Hardyman, Robyn.
Title: Skyscrapers / Robyn Hardyman.
Description: New York : PowerKids Press, 2017. | Series: Engineering eurekas | Includes index.
Identifiers: ISBN 9781499431056 (pbk.) | ISBN 9781499431070 (library bound) | ISBN 9781499431063 (6 pack)
Subjects: LCSH: Skyscrapers--Juvenile literature.
Classification: LCC NA6230.H349 2017 | DDC 720'.483--dc23

Copyright © 2017 by The Rosen Publishing Group

Produced for Rosen by Calcium Creative Ltd
Editors for Calcium Creative Ltd: Sarah Eason and Harriet McGregor
Designers: Paul Myerscough and Jessica Moon
Picture researcher: Rachel Blount

Picture credits: Cover: Shutterstock: Badahos. Inside: Venetia Dean artwork 29; Shutterstock: Arndale 20, AvDe 27, Robert Paul Van Beets 16–17, Ana del Castillo 4–5c, Richard Cavalleri 18, DW labs Incorporated 6–7, Everett Historical 13l, F11photo 10–11c, Julien Hautcoeur 9r, Patricia Hofmeester 11c, IndustryAndTravel 23r, Sophie James 22–23c, Brian Kinney 5r, Jeffrey Liao 21l, Meunierd 3, 12–13c, Naufal MQ 28, Noppasin 21r, Phant 15r, Sergio TB 13r, TungCheung 19, Leonard Zhukovsky 17r; Adrian Smith + Gordon Gill Architecture: © Jeddah Economic Company/Adrian Smith + Gordon Gill Architecture - Design Architects of the project; Wikimedia Commons: Chicago Architectural Photographing Company 8–9c, The Pictorial News Co., N.Y. 11r, Stevecadman 1, 14–15.

All rights reserved. No part of this book may be reproduced in any form without permission in writing from the publisher, except by a reviewer.

Manufactured in the United States of America
CPSIA Compliance Information: Batch #BW17PK: For Further Information contact Rosen Publishing, New York, New York at 1-800-237-9932.

Contents

Amazing Engineering 4
How to Ascend 6
Iron and Steel 8
The Home of the Skyscraper 10
Higher and Higher 12
Walls of Glass 14
A New Structure 16
Technical Innovations 18
The Race to the Sky 20
How Far Can We Go? 22
Global Skyscrapers 24
Skyscrapers of the Future 26
Symbols of Progress 28
Glossary 30
Further Reading 31
Index 32

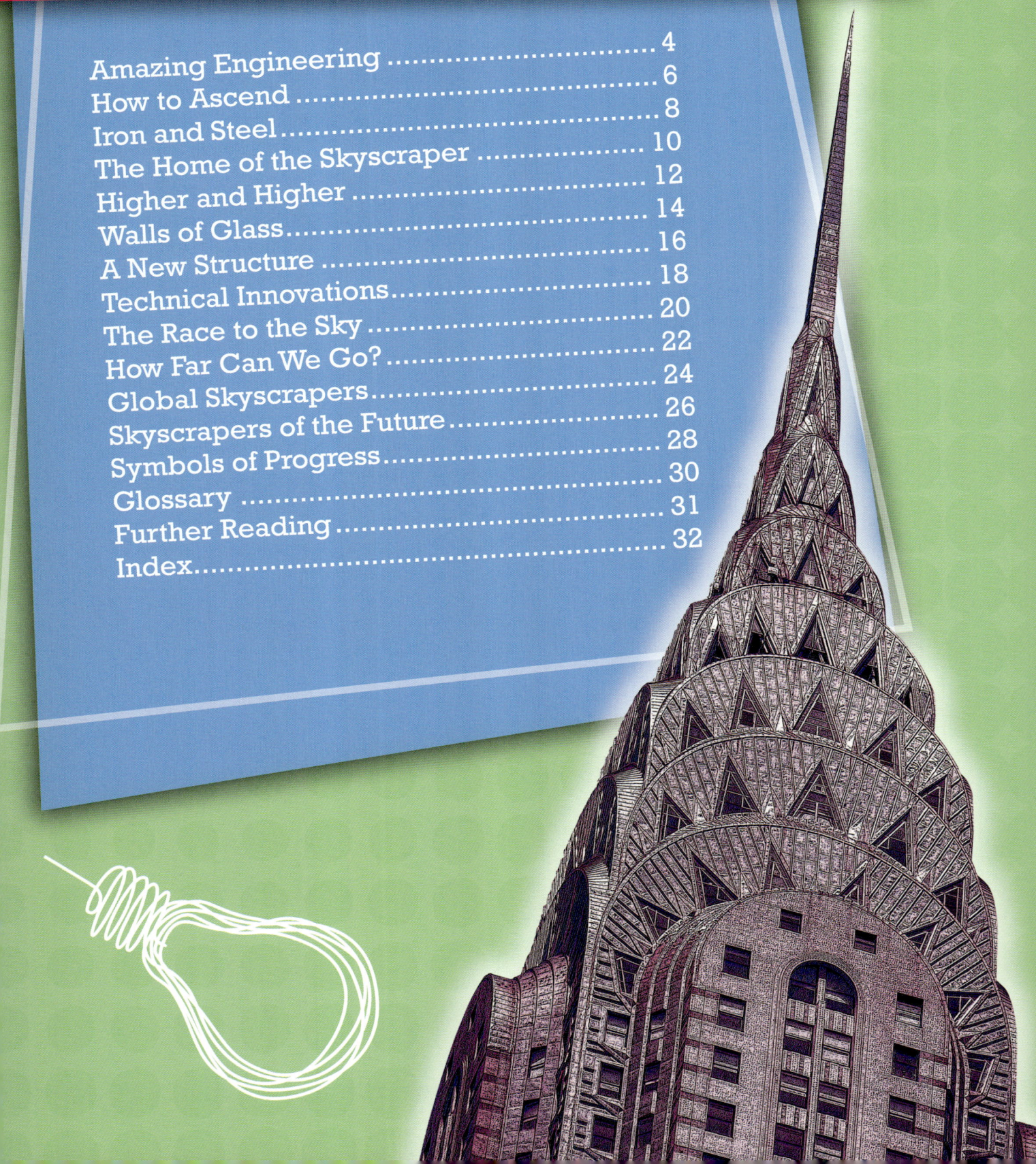

Amazing Engineering

Throughout history, people have wanted to build big. The ancient Egyptians built huge pyramids, and as our cities have grown, we have made churches and towers that reach farther and farther up into the sky. Until about 150 years ago, we could build only with stone and brick. These materials are heavy. To support the walls and floors the buildings had to be massive at the base and limited in height. Then, in the nineteenth century, came a whole new type of building, the skyscraper.

Historic Heights

For many hundreds of years the only tall buildings in most places were churches, temples, and castles. They were built of stone and could be surprisingly high. When the cathedral at Beauvais, in France, was built in the thirteenth century, it was the tallest in the world. Inside it was 157.5 feet (48 m) high.

A 15-story building could have fit inside Beauvais Cathedral.

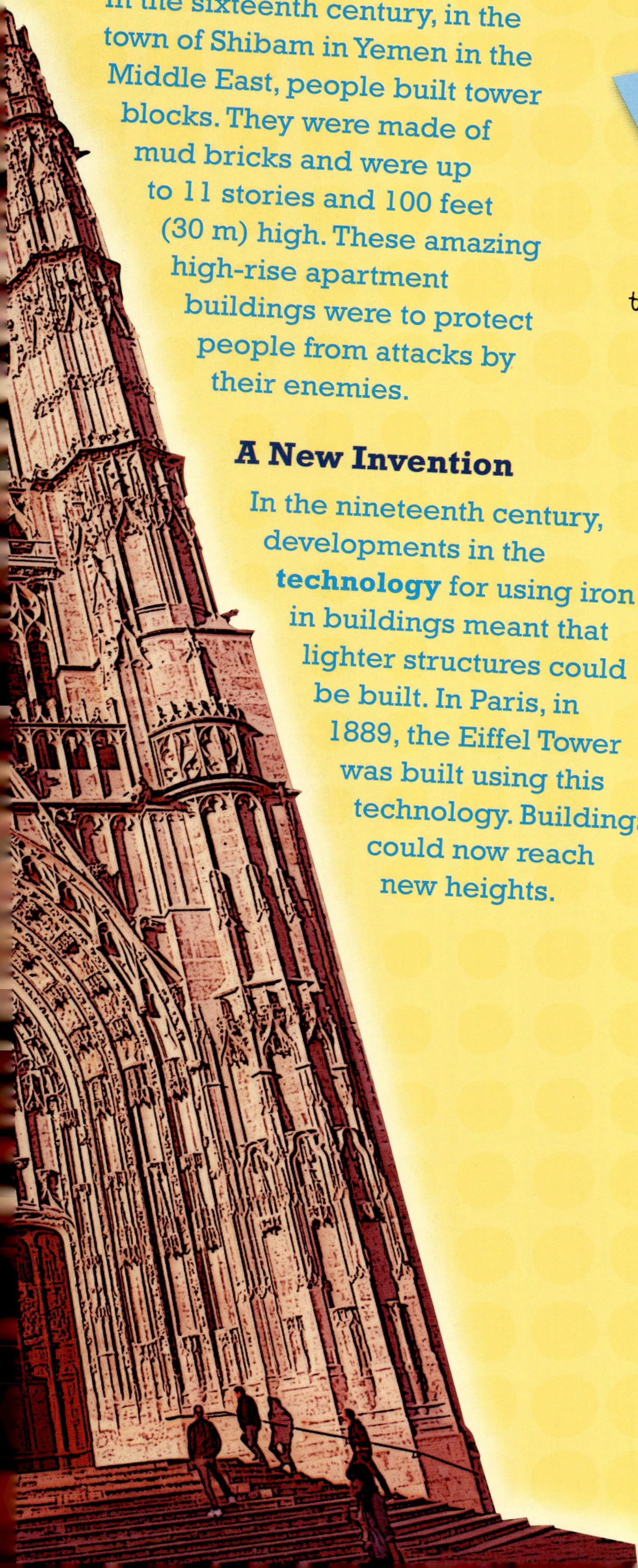

In the sixteenth century, in the town of Shibam in Yemen in the Middle East, people built tower blocks. They were made of mud bricks and were up to 11 stories and 100 feet (30 m) high. These amazing high-rise apartment buildings were to protect people from attacks by their enemies.

ENGINEERING FIRSTS

At 986 feet (300.5 m), the Eiffel Tower was the tallest structure in the world until 1930.

A New Invention

In the nineteenth century, developments in the **technology** for using iron in buildings meant that lighter structures could be built. In Paris, in 1889, the Eiffel Tower was built using this technology. Buildings could now reach new heights.

Frenchman Alexandre Gustave Eiffel (1832–1923) was a famous **engineer**. He designed many large railways bridges and buildings, and the frame that supported the Statue of Liberty in New York City. He was one of the first people to make strong but light structures from iron. The iron beams in the Eiffel Tower were all joined by millions of pins called **rivets**.

How to Ascend

The **Industrial Revolution** in the nineteenth century made it possible for engineers to explore building high with first iron and then **steel**. If buildings were to have many more stories, however, there was a major problem to be solved. How would people get up and down inside them? No one wanted to climb dozens of flights of stairs.

Going Up

Steam-powered **elevators** had been around since the early nineteenth century. However, they were designed to move materials and were not always safe for people to use. The cables that held them could break. In a tall building, that would send people falling to their deaths. In 1853, an American inventor named Elisha Graves Otis (1811–1861) figured out how to make an elevator that was safe for people. If the cable snapped, a wooden frame on top of the elevator car would hit the walls of the shaft and catch in a groove. This kept the car from falling.

FUTURE EUREKAS!

The company that Elisha Otis began, Otis Elevators, is still in business today. It is part of an industry figuring out how to make elevators faster and safer for the skyscrapers of the future. Its double-decker elevator in the Burj Khalifa building (completed in 2009) travels at almost 22 miles (35 km) per hour.

First Elevator

In fact, the first elevator shaft was put into a building before Otis had designed his safe system. In 1853, Peter Cooper (1791–1883) was confident that a safe elevator would soon be designed. He had a shaft built into his building, the Cooper Union Foundation in New York City. Cooper was right, and Otis did eventually install a safe elevator in the building.

From the 1880s onward, elevators were powered by electricity. That meant there was nothing to keep engineers and architects from designing many more spectacular tall buildings.

Today the Cooper Union Building in New York City is a center of learning for engineers and **architects**.

Iron and Steel

The major **innovation** that made skyscrapers possible was a structural frame made of steel. This was much lighter than stone or bricks. In a stone or brick building, the walls support the weight of the building. In a steel-frame building, the skeleton frame supports all the weight of the walls and floors, and all the building's contents.

A Growing City

In the 1880s, the city of Chicago, Illinois, was growing fast. When the Home Insurance Company decided to build a new headquarters, they wanted it to be tall. The competition to design and build it was won by an engineer named William LeBaron Jenney (1832–1907). For the first time, he proposed a 10-story building constructed around an iron frame. It would be covered in stone on the outside to keep out wind and rain, and would be fireproof. During building, construction work on the project was stopped to check that the building really would stand up on its own. Then, Jenney got the idea to switch from using iron to steel for the frame. This new, better material was much stronger than iron.

The Home Insurance Building in Chicago was completed in 1885. It was the world's first skyscraper. This landmark building also had the first safety elevators, fireproofing, and electrical wiring.

ENGINEERING FIRSTS

Chicago remained an important center for developments in skyscraper design.

In 1885, the completed Home Insurance Building, in Chicago, Illinois, weighed only one-third as much as it would have in stone.

After the Home Insurance Building was completed, a group of architects and engineers in Chicago worked together to develop this new engineering technology further. They were known as the Chicago School. They changed the way that cities were built, upward rather than outward. From now on the sky was, quite literally, the limit.

The Home of the Skyscraper

Once the idea of building with steel beams had been tried, it took off fast. In New York City land was in short supply, so it was valuable. The way to make best use of it was to build upward. In the early years of the twentieth century, many famous skyscrapers were built in New York City. As the technology improved, the buildings grew higher and higher!

Fantastic Flatiron

One of the first New York City skyscrapers was the Flatiron Building, which opened in 1902. This strange building was on a corner plot, so it was built in the shape of a triangle! It has 21 stories and is 307 feet (87 m) high. The outside is made of stone, but inside is a skeleton of steel. Because it rises straight up from the street, instead of standing on a wider base, people at the time thought it would fall down. However, it is still standing today.

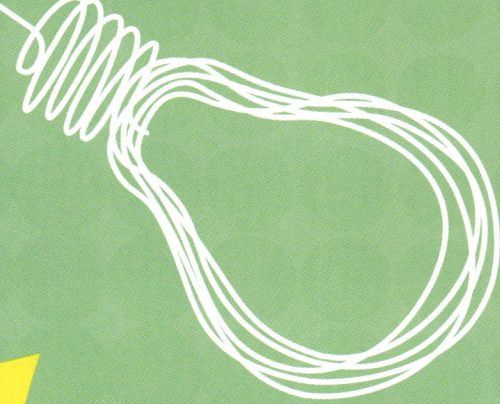

At its narrow end, the Flatiron Building is only 6 feet (1.8 m) wide.

The Singer Building

The Singer Building went up next, in 1907. The building was narrow but high. It had 47 stories so it needed very deep **foundations** and extra protection against the wind. The narrow tower was set back from the street on a lower but wider base. This kept the building from darkening the street outside.

ENGINEERING FIRSTS

The Singer Building (shown here) was demolished in 1967, to make way for a bigger skyscraper.

The Woolworth Building's steel frame weighed 49,600 tons (45,000 mt). The builders worked high up on the beams with no scaffolding!

The Woolworth Building was built in New York City in 1913. It had 57 stories. It was the tallest building in the world until 1930. Its owner wanted it to look like a medieval cathedral, so it was covered with decorative stonework. The entrance lobby was made three stories high. It also had 5,000 windows to let in a lot of light.

Higher and Higher

In New York City in 1929, a race began to build the tallest skyscraper in the world. The Bank of Manhattan Trust Company and Walter Chrysler (1875–1940), a wealthy businessman in the car industry, were both building new skyscrapers. They both wanted to win the race. Soon they would be outranked by a truly incredible structure.

Learning by Building

Engineers were improving steel frame structures so these amazing new buildings could go higher and higher. They were also developing faster methods of construction, so they could go up in just 12 months. Teams of thousands of men could construct four stories every week. In the spring of 1930, it seemed as if the Bank of Manhattan's building would be the tallest. Then, a thin spire was raised from inside the Chrysler Building at the last minute. At 1,046 feet (319 m), it was the world's tallest building.

The Chrysler Building was decorated with metal hubcaps and other ornaments from cars, to help promote the business.

Record Breaker

In April 1931, after just 410 days of construction, a new champion building was completed in New York City. It was officially opened when President Herbert Hoover (1874–1964) turned on the building's lights with the flick of a switch from Washington, DC. The Empire State Building was 1,250 feet (381 m) high and remained the tallest building in the world until 1972. However, the steel frame meant that there were no open, **column**-free spaces inside the building.

ENGINEERING FIRSTS

The steel framework of the Empire State Building weighed 60,000 tons (54,430 mt). The building had 6,500 windows.

There are 73 elevators inside the Empire State Building.

The Empire State Building was the first to have more than 100 stories (it had 102). It was also designed to be a lightning rod for the area, to carry electricity from lightning into the ground.

Walls of Glass

From the 1930s, skyscrapers went up in many of the great cities of the world. As they grew taller, they needed to be even stronger and lighter. Engineers were looking for new materials to achieve this. One was glass.

Mies van der Rohe

In 1921, a German architect named Mies van der Rohe (1886–1969) designed a skyscraper for the city of Berlin, in Germany. He used a new material: the walls of his building were made of glass. For the first time, there was no structural or decorative stone. The building was never constructed, however, and it was not until the 1940s and 1950s that glass was used in this way. Van der Rohe moved to the United States. In 1958, his astonishing new Seagram Building in New York City changed forever the way skyscrapers look.

The Seagram Building used glass and metal instead of stone and brick to cover its steel frame.

Seagram Building

Mies van der Rohe believed skyscrapers should look "minimalist." They should have little decoration and high standards of building, even down to the smallest details. The beauty of the basic structure should be clear for all to see, and the inside of the building should be full of light. The Seagram Building achieved all of this. Another innovation was to set it back from the street, with an open plaza in front. This allowed light to reach down to street level and meant people could view the building more easily. A new modern age in skyscraper design had begun.

ENGINEERING FIRSTS

Derzhprom in Kharkiv, Ukraine, was a radical sight at the time and many tourists visited it.

The first European skyscraper complex was Derzhprom. It was built in Kharkiv, Ukraine, in 1928. In a large circular plaza stand three clusters of towers made of concrete and glass. **Skybridges**, several stories high and lined with windows, connect the buildings.

A New Structure

As skyscrapers grew taller, they began to face a new problem: the wind. When strong winds hit the side of a skyscraper, the steel columns on that side stretch apart. The columns on the other side squeeze together. Buildings were beginning to sway! If buildings were going to rise higher, the engineers needed a new solution.

A Tubular Solution

At first, the solution was to strengthen the core, or center, of the building. The steel columns and beams were located at the center, creating a core that could withstand the wind. This also meant there was more open space inside that could be used.

The second solution was much more revolutionary. It moved the columns and beams from the inside of the building to the outside edges. There they were positioned close together. This made the building into a stiff tube with open space in the middle. It was as strong as the core design, but much lighter because it used less steel. The tube construction meant that buildings could be taller. From the 1960s, most skyscrapers more than 40 stories high used this design.

The best-known example of tube construction was the World Trade Center in New York City. It was completed in 1972-1973. Each tower had 110 stories.

ENGINEERING FIRSTS

In the John Hancock Center, Chicago, the "X" design is essential to its engineering but it also looks attractive.

The creator of the tube-like design in skyscrapers was Fazlur Khan (1929–1982), an American structural engineer born in Bangladesh. His design innovations revolutionized high-rise buildings and led to a huge increase in skyscraper construction around the world. Khan also invented the "trussed tube" design, in which huge "X" steel structures are part of the building's engineering. He first used it in the John Hancock Center in Chicago, Illinois, completed in 1967–1970.

Technical Innovations

Now that skyscrapers could safely be higher, there were many other aspects of building them that needed engineering innovation. Some were about building more interesting shapes. Some were about building faster, to cut costs. Others were about the best way to use the space inside.

Not Just a Box

In 1974, a new skyscraper became the tallest building in the world. It was the Sears Tower (now known as the Willis Tower) in Chicago, Illinois. The tower is 1,730 feet (520 m) tall, including the antennae on its roof. The roof is 1,450 feet (442 m) high. The tower was remarkable not only for its height but also for its tubular structure, which allows different building shapes to be grouped together. The tubular design meant the skyscraper no longer had to be simply a rectangular box.

The Sears Tower in Chicago, Illinois, was the first skyscraper to be more than a tall, thin box.

The Need for Speed

As skyscrapers got bigger, the costs of building them grew too. This drove the invention of faster and cheaper construction methods. The new Hong Kong and Shanghai Bank (HSBC) headquarters in Hong Kong were completed in 1986. Many of the building's parts were **prefabricated**. This meant they were made elsewhere and brought to the site to be assembled. Flooring panels came from the United States and steel compartments from Scotland. **Service pods** came from Japan and other parts came from places around the world.

FUTURE EUREKAS!

Prefabrication methods have since been developed further. The tallest new buildings today use this technology to keep costs down. Engineers are working on it all the time so the tallest buildings of the future can go up in record time.

Getting Around

To keep elevators from taking up too much space, fewer, faster elevators took people to a certain level. There, in a **sky lobby**, they could transfer either to a slow elevator to travel a few stories or another fast one to reach the next sky lobby. With this system, elevators used about 70 percent less space. Escalators were also developed for the new, more open interior spaces.

The HSBC Bank's building in Hong Kong had the longest freely supported escalators in the world.

The Race to the Sky

The Sears Tower in Chicago, Illinois, held the record as the world's tallest building for more than 20 years. Finally, in 1998, the record went to a new skyscraper. This time, for the first time, it was not in the United States.

Petronas Towers

The Petronas Towers were completed in Kuala Lumpur, Malaysia, in 1998. At 1,483 feet (452 m) and 88 stories, with 32,000 windows, this pair of towers was impressive. They were built using high-strength **reinforced concrete**. This material is also effective in keeping the building stable in high winds. One new feature of these skyscrapers was that they were not rectangular. Each tower was built in the shape of an eight-pointed star. This is an **Islamic** decorative shape.

It took almost 37,000 tons (33,570 mt) of steel to build the Petronas Towers.

Taipei 101

In 2004, Taipei 101 in Taiwan took the height record, at 1,670 feet (509 m) and 101 stories. Engineers designed it to withstand even the typhoons and earthquakes that are common in the region. It is one of the most stable buildings ever constructed. It has very deep foundations, a massive concrete core, and steel columns on the outside. Its most amazing feature is a heavy swinging **pendulum** near the top. The pendulum moves in high winds to reduce the amount of sway in the building. This is called a **tuned mass damper.**

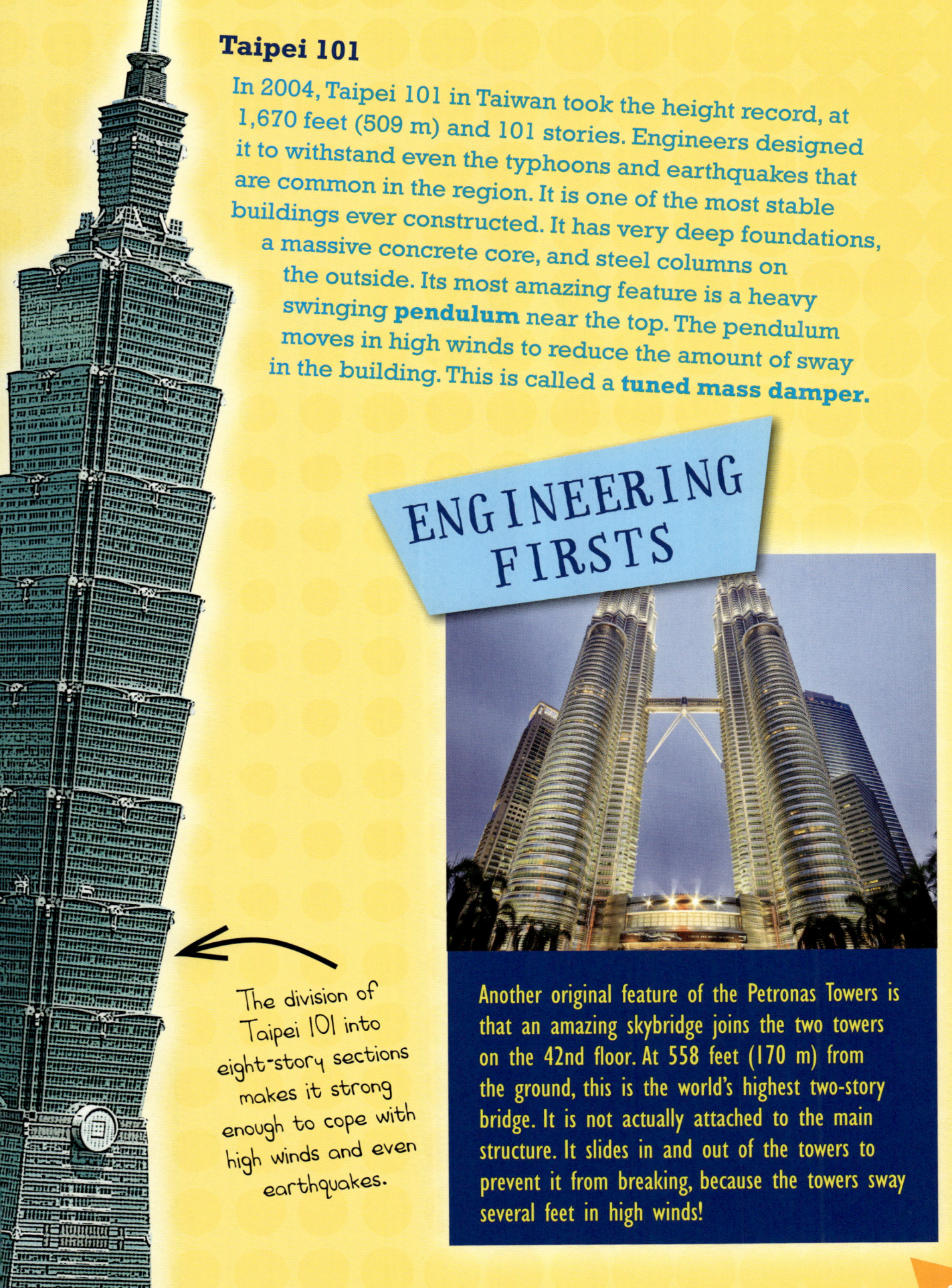

The division of Taipei 101 into eight-story sections makes it strong enough to cope with high winds and even earthquakes.

ENGINEERING FIRSTS

Another original feature of the Petronas Towers is that an amazing skybridge joins the two towers on the 42nd floor. At 558 feet (170 m) from the ground, this is the world's highest two-story bridge. It is not actually attached to the main structure. It slides in and out of the towers to prevent it from breaking, because the towers sway several feet in high winds!

How Far Can We Go?

In the twenty-first century, engineers and architects around the world have created new styles for skyscrapers. They are reaching ever higher, in new designs that are a long way from the traditional rectangular box. They often reflect the **culture** of their location.

Breaking the Rules

In 2010, on the edge of the desert in Dubai in the United Arab Emirates, a new skyscraper opened. It is almost double the height of the Empire State Building. This is Burj Khalifa. It stands 2,722 feet (829.8 m) high and has 163 stories. The shape of the building is based on the local desert flower, *Hymenocallis*. Its American architect was Adrian Smith (born in 1944), who designed it from his offices in a 1911 Chicago skyscraper.

ENGINEERING FIRSTS

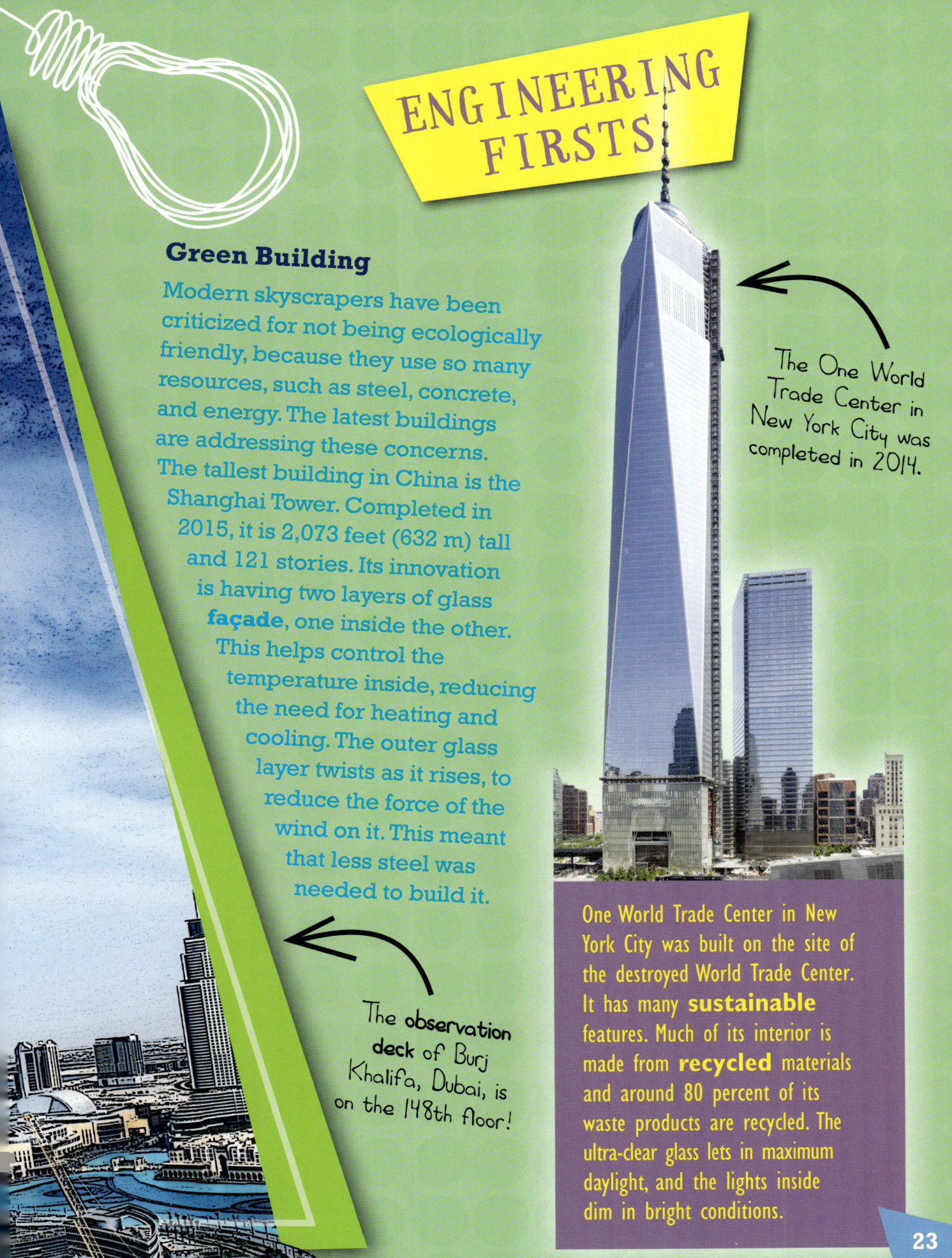

Green Building

Modern skyscrapers have been criticized for not being ecologically friendly, because they use so many resources, such as steel, concrete, and energy. The latest buildings are addressing these concerns. The tallest building in China is the Shanghai Tower. Completed in 2015, it is 2,073 feet (632 m) tall and 121 stories. Its innovation is having two layers of glass **façade**, one inside the other. This helps control the temperature inside, reducing the need for heating and cooling. The outer glass layer twists as it rises, to reduce the force of the wind on it. This meant that less steel was needed to build it.

The One World Trade Center in New York City was completed in 2014.

The **observation deck** of Burj Khalifa, Dubai, is on the 148th floor!

One World Trade Center in New York City was built on the site of the destroyed World Trade Center. It has many **sustainable** features. Much of its interior is made from **recycled** materials and around 80 percent of its waste products are recycled. The ultra-clear glass lets in maximum daylight, and the lights inside dim in bright conditions.

Global Skyscrapers

If you could visit any skyscraper in the world, which would you pick and why?

Willis Tower, Chicago, Illinois, 1,730 feet (520 m)

The Shard, London, UK, 1,016 feet (310 m), tallest in UK

NORTH AMERICA

EUROPE

Torre de Cristal, Madrid, Spain, 817 feet (249 m), tallest in Spain

US Bank Tower, Los Angeles, 1,018 feet (310 m)

One World Trade Center, New York City, 1,791 feet (546 m)

AFRICA

SOUTH AMERICA

How do engineers make skyscrapers strong enough to rise so high? How do skyscrapers withstand earthquakes and high winds?

How do you think skyscrapers improve a city? Why might they make the people who live there feel proud?

Gran Torre Santiago, Santiago, Chile, 980 feet (300 m)

If you could design a new skyscraper for a city near you, what features would you include? What materials would you use? What designs would suit your city's culture and history?

Federation Tower, Moscow, Russia, 1,226 feet (374 m), tallest in Europe

Shanghai Tower, Shanghai, China, 2,073 feet (632 m)

Guangzhou Twin Towers, Guangzhou, China, 1,740 feet (530 m) and 1,439 feet (439 m)

ASIA

Taipei 101, Taipei, Taiwan, 1,670 feet (509 m)

Burj Khalifa, Dubai, United Arab Emirates, 2,722 feet (829.8 m)

Petronas Towers, Kuala Lumpur, Malaysia, 1,483 feet (452 m)

Queensland Number One, Gold Coast, Australia, 1,058 feet (322 m), tallest in the southern hemisphere

AUSTRALIA

Carlton Centre, Johannesburg, South Africa, 732 feet (223 m)

Do you think skyscrapers are a good way to deal with the problem of lack of space in cities? Do their advantages outweigh their disadvantages? Give evidence to support your answer.

Skyscrapers of the Future

The first skyscrapers were built in cities where land was in short supply. Many of the newest are being built in areas where there is little development, such as the edges of the desert. These "trophy" skyscrapers are designed to attract new development around them after they are built. With each one, the engineering breaks through new barriers in innovation.

The Ultimate Skyscraper?

In 2020, a new skyscraper will be completed that will be an engineering landmark. The Jeddah Tower in Saudi Arabia will be the first to rise more than 3,280 feet (1 km) into the sky. The Y-shaped base of the building will give it stability against the wind. The triangular core at its center will give it strength. Its sloped outside surface will be made of the latest heat-reflecting glass, and its elevators will use new **carbon fiber** technology to go higher than ever before. A circular sky terrace, or platform, will stick out at 2,000 feet (610 m). The cost of this giant will be $1.23 billion.

The Jeddah Tower is designed to represent a bundle of leaves shooting up from the ground.

Faster and Faster

One of the biggest innovations in skyscraper engineering is in the speed of construction. In 2015, a Chinese company built a 57-story building in just 19 days. Almost all the building's parts were prefabricated in a factory, and assembled on site. With traditional construction methods it would have taken two years.

FUTURE EUREKAS!

The number of stories an elevator can travel has always been limited by the strength and weight of its steel cables. Now, builders are using a new kind of cable. It has stronger but lighter carbon fibers and will be able to take a single elevator up twice as many stories, up to 3,280 feet (1 km) at a time.

In the future, elevators will be able to travel farther and faster.

Symbols of Progress

Ever since people learned to make buildings with a framework of steel, they have longed to build them higher and higher. Once engineers mastered the art of building tall boxes, they turned to making skyscrapers more varied in shape. They also began to design buildings that related to the culture of their location. Through all of this, they were figuring out new ways to overcome the problems of building so high.

Symbols of Power

Today's skyscrapers are symbols of power, wealth, progress, and hope for the future. Some are built in the heart of busy cities. Others stand alone, waiting for the land around them to catch up. Architects and engineers around the world are making the best use of valuable land to create the beautiful, innovative, sustainable skyscrapers of the future.

These "cities in the sky" are wonders of engineering.

How High Is Too High?

Engineers think it is possible to build a skyscraper 1 mile (1.6 km) high, with new innovations in design and materials. The question, however, is whether there would ever be a demand for such a building. Although our growing population will always need places to live, work, and relax, some people think our taste for these extreme "cities in the sky" has reached its limit. What do you think?

Be an Engineer

Engineers learn from experience to see what kinds of structures are strongest. How tall a tower can you build using newspaper? Follow these steps to find out!

You Will Need:
- Two sheets of newspaper
- Adhesive tape
- A table

- You can fold or tear the paper however you want.
- First, try making a tower with a single newspaper tube. How tall can it be before it falls?
- Can you make a stronger tower by using more paper tubes?
- You can test your tower against the wind by blowing on it. Earthquake-test it by gently shaking the table.

Glossary

architects Building designers.

carbon fiber An extremely strong and lightweight material.

column A vertical support structure often used in buildings.

culture The customs and traditions of a group of people.

elevators Devices for taking people or goods from one level to another inside a building.

engineer A person who uses science to design structures.

façade The outside surface of a building.

foundations The part of a building below ground level that supports its weight.

Industrial Revolution A period of time in which goods began to be made using machinery instead of by hand.

innovation A new thing.

Islamic Having to do with Islam, the religion of Muslims.

observation deck A place high on a skyscraper where people can see the view.

pendulum A weight hung from a fixed support so it swings by gravity.

prefabricated Made in a factory to be assembled on site.

recycled Changed into material that can be used again.

reinforced concrete Concrete with pieces of steel in it to make it stronger.

rivets Metal pins used to join two pieces of metal.

service pods Special areas for food or maintenance.

skybridges Bridges between two parts of a skyscraper, at a high level.

sky lobby A floor in a skyscraper where people can transfer from the fast elevators to the more local elevators.

steel A strong metal made from iron and carbon.

sustainable Built and maintained with little impact on the natural environment.

technology The tools and methods used to solve the problems of how things work.

tuned mass damper A pendulum used to prevent sway in very tall skyscrapers.

Further Reading

Books

Cornille, Didier. *Who Built That? Skyscrapers*. New York, NY: Princeton Architectural Press, 2014.

Finger, Brad. *13 Skyscrapers Children Should Know*. New York, NY: Prestel, 2016.

Malam, John. *You Wouldn't Want to Be a Skyscraper Builder!* St. Louis, MO: Turtleback, 2009.

Shea, Therese. *How a Skyscraper Is Built*. New York, NY: Gareth Stevens, 2016.

Websites

Due to the changing nature of Internet links, PowerKids Press has developed an online list of websites related to the subject of this book. This site is updated regularly. Please use this link to access the list:

www.powerkidslinks.com/ee/skyscrapers

Index

A
architects, 7, 9, 14, 22, 28

B
Burj Khalifa, 7, 22, 25

C
Chrysler Building, 12
Chrysler, Walter, 12
column, 13, 16, 21
concrete, 15, 20–21, 23
Cooper Union Foundation, 7
Cooper, Peter, 7
costs, 18–19, 26

E
Eiffel Tower, 5
Eiffel, Alexandre Gustave, 5
elevators, 6–7, 9, 19, 26–27
Empire State Building, 13, 22
engineer, 5–9, 12, 14, 16–17, 19, 21–22, 24, 28–29

F
Flatiron Building, 10
foundations, 11, 21

G
glass, 14, 15, 23, 26

H
Home Insurance Building, 9
Hoover, Herbert, 13

I
Industrial Revolution, 6

J
Jeddah Tower, 26
Jenney, William LeBaron, 8
John Hancock Center, 17

K
Khan, Fazlur, 17

O
One World Trade Center, 23–24
Otis Elevators, 7
Otis, Elisha Graves, 6–7

P
Petronas Towers, 20–21, 25

S
Seagram Building, 14–15
Sears Tower (Willis Tower), 18, 20, 24
Shanghai Tower, 23, 25
Singer Building, 11
skybridges, 15, 21
sky lobby, 19
Smith, Adrian, 22
Statue of Liberty, 5
steel, 6, 8, 10, 12–13, 16–17, 19, 21, 23, 27–28

T
Taipei 101, 21, 25

V
van der Rohe, Mies, 14–15

W
Woolworth Building, 11